The Oratory]

(for use with congregation/u

Kyrie

MATTHEW MARTIN

4

Lord,___ have mer - cy,

Lord, have mer - cy.

Gloria

King,___ O___ God, al - might - y Fa - ther.

più f legato

f

Man.

mf

Lord, Je - sus Christ,___

legato

mf

Ped.

on - ly be - got - ten Son.___ Lord God, Lamb of God, Son___ of the

Fa - ther, you take a - way the sins of the world, have mer - cy___ up -

Sanctus and Benedictus*

Ho - ly, ho - ly, ho - ly, Lord God of hosts, hea-ven and earth are full of your glo - ry. Ho - san - na in the high - est. Bless - ed is he who comes in the name of the Lord.

* please see page 9 for higher version

Ho - san - na in__ the high - est.

Agnus Dei

♩ = c.76

Lamb of__God, you take a - way the__

mp legato

Ped.

sins of the world, have mer - cy up - on us.

poco cresc.

Lamb of__God, you take a - way the__ sins of the world, have

mer - cy up - on us. Lamb of__ God, you take a - way__ the__

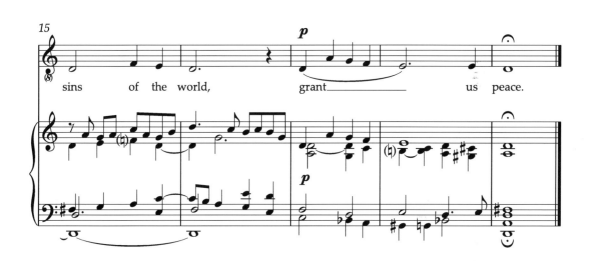

sins of the world, grant_____ us peace.

Sanctus and Benedictus

alternative version in C

Ho - ly, ho - ly, ho - ly,

Man.   Ped.

Return to page 8 for the Agnus Dei

WORKS INCLUDE:

The Faber Choral Signature Series introduces a wealth of new or recently written choral music to choirs in search of fresh repertoire. The series draws in a rich diversity of contemporary composers and includes both lighter and more challenging works, offering a thrilling array of varied styles.

Commissioned by The Oratory School, Woodcote for the 2016 Conference of Catholic School Directors of Music, this congregational mass for unison voices is a joyful and uplifting setting, suitable for all voices and abilities. A separate four page part for the congregation is also available for download.

MATTHEW MARTIN was born in 1976 and studied at Magdalen College, Oxford and the Royal Academy of Music. He is regularly commissioned to write music for leading ensembles and festivals, most recently the BBC Singers, the Cardinall's Musick, the choirs of Westminster Abbey, St Paul's Cathedral and St John's College, Cambridge, the St David's Cathedral Festival and the American Guild of Organists.

Photo © Simon Tottman

For a full listing of works, to peruse scores and listen to recordings, go to
www.choralstore.com

Join our on-line choral community:
www.facebook.com/choralstore   Twitter: @choralstore

ISBN10:   0-571-53976-9
EAN13:   978-0-571-53976-5

FABER *ff* MUSIC

fabermusic.com

9 780571 539765